WALLS THAT I CANNOT BREAK

How to heal a broken heart and move forward to establish healthy, fulfilled relationships.

Eugenia Lartey-Attigah, LPC, NCC.

Forward

This book is dedicated to my late father Emmanuel Larte Lartey. He instilled in me the essence of hard work ethic and determination, and the importance of pursuing higher education. My mother, Elizabeth Lartey for her wisdom and tough love. My twin sister, Patricia Lartey, for her support, encouragement and "Twin battles." A special thank you-- to my other five brothers and sisters and nine nieces and one nephew for motivating me to be a better person. To my best friends: Missy, Patrice, Renae, Coretta, I appreciate you for checking in with me and making sure I am okay. To my work bae, Ms. Juanese Moore, I appreciate your "Taurus hardcore truth" for encouraging me to critically think through issues that I personally and professionally face.

Dr. Russell Floyd and Mrs. Denise Floyd, my adopted father and mother, I thank you for the long walks in the park and pushing me beyond my comfort zone and telling me that my research paper suck, so that I can revise it and get a better grade! Every person in this life needs a backbone, and I just want to thank Mr. Antonio Smith and his family for being that for me. World Changers Nation and Life Bridge Church, I appreciate your ministries for spiritually pouring into me. I want to say a special thank you to every client I have ever worked with. I appreciate the fact that you trust me with your life and in the gifting that God has placed on my life.

Table of Contents

Chapter 1
Self -Awareness

"Knowledge is information and wisdom are knowledge in action"

Self-awareness: conscious knowledge of one's own character, feelings, motives, and desires.

Self-Awareness is essential to the first step of the healing process. However, the lack of self - awareness can cause an individual to destroy particularly important relationships. Often, when individuals have been hurt, most of the time people unconsciously keep the score of disappointment, fear, hurt, and psychological pain completed at the hands of our family members, friends, and partners. In future relationships, there may be a manifestation of the pain, which may appear as anger, irritability, or emotional coldness. An individual who lacks self - awareness will be easily triggered by the actions of their mate, friend/ co-worker, and their reaction to their trigger will be the actions of a friend or loved one that is so intense that it may scare people or sabotage meaningful relationships.

Therefore, it is important that you self-reflect and look at your life. Have you been through a traumatic experience? Are there patterns of the same issue, but different partner? Are you alone and frustrated about how your life is going? In the book, "**The Clarity Cleanse**" 12 Steps to Finding Renewed Energy, Spiritual Fulfillment, and Emotional Healing Dr. Habib Sadeghi discussed how the human mind deals with emotional triggers. Dr. Sadeghi stated that when someone puts pressure on an emotional wound, the natural human reaction is to respond defensively, which is projective identification. However, people have a right to an opinion. If we are emotionally healed, their words would not affect us. If we are still wounded, their words will affect us. Therefore, we must apply loving-kindness to those wounded areas to allow them to heal. Once you can identify, what the root cause is; you can start the process of healing the soul's wound. According to Eduardo Duran, a well-respected multi-cultural mental health expert, he describes a soul wound from an American Indian Perspective. A soul wound develops when recent or past historic life event occurred and fractured the harmonious interconnection between the mind, body, and spirit. Metaphorically, can you imagine a person having fresh bleeding, raw wound on their heart that is my depiction of a soul wound? Moreover, people can see physically wounds, but often people cannot see emotional pain because we use a mask to disguise our truth. When an individual has true self -awareness, an individual can effectively communicate with the people they love their emotions and how their actions are affecting them. Also, an individual with self- awareness can admit when they have overacted to a situation based on past experiences. What goes hand in hand with self-awareness is self-love.

Self-Reflection Questions

1. Do you have self-awareness?
2. Has anyone ever addressed your behavior patterns, if so, what was your response?
3. How can you apply having self-awareness to your life in this present moment?

Journal Entry

Chapter 2

Self- Love

Self- Love: Self-love is regarding one's own well-being and happiness.

"How you love yourself is how you teach people to treat you"

In my opinion, I believe that self-love is the highest expression of love. I personally had to learn what that was in my own life. I found myself wanting to please people and make sure they were okay at the expense of my happiness. I am a work in progress and I have implemented some effective communication and coping skills that I would like to share with you. First, please make sure that you learn how to say "No"! Often, we show people how to treat us, so what happens when your "No" has no power? People are always used to you saying yes. I dare you to do something different— it may feel a little weird. However, you will get past feeling guilty and it will start to feel empowering. Remember to add balance in everything you do! Secondly, speak your truth. In working with my clients, if I am working with someone, who is angry? Once we start to unravel the surface emotions, the client will communicate all these secondary, underlying emotions such as hurt, frustration, fear. I always ask did you tell the person how you felt, and I get a resounding "No!" Therefore, it is so important to speak what is on your heart because if you do not, it will literally hurt you. Lastly, speak life into your life. If you are dealing with something negative and difficult, what are you saying about the situation? The power of verbal affirmations can change your life. There is a difference between head knowledge and heart knowledge. You can say something and you can remember it by heart; however, there is something about when you meditate on inspirational word and you believe it, that's when it becomes heart knowledge and that's when things will change in your life. For example, I was scared to drive, but I had enough faith to believe God for a car. The scripture that I meditated on was Hebrews 11:1 (KJV) "Now, faith is the substance of things hoped for with the evidence of things not seen". I could see the fact that I did not have any driver's license, no car, but in the spirit, I saw that car in the driveway, so every time I walk home from work. I would point at the ground and I say car manifest in Jesus name. Three months later, I got my driver's license and a debt-free car. I dare you to try God and speak the word of God! It works!

Self- Reflection Questions

1. What is your definition of self-love?
2. What happens when your "No" has no power?
3. How can you apply faith to a negative situation that you are facing right now?

Journal Entry

Chapter 3

Do you have a wall or a boundary up?

"Setting appropriate boundaries is an act of self-care"

Wall: A continuous vertical brick or stone structure that encloses or divides an area of land.

Psychological Boundary: is anything that marks a limit between behavior that does cause emotional harm and behavior that does not cause emotional harm.

If you are a client of mine, I have a question that I ask anyone that sees me about unforgiveness. Are you operating from a wall or a boundary? Often, I get this look from my client like a deer in headlights and a silence renders the room. Which I love because I see the client is in deep thought. The answer is usually a "Wall." Here is the issue with a wall, you can potentially miss out on some amazing people. You rob humanity of your personality, your sense of humor, your smile when you operate from a wall. You remove the two bricks, and the only thing people see is your eyes. I want to be clear that I am very understanding of emotional and physical trauma and distress. Therefore, I encourage you to seek mental health counseling to process your past so, you can deal with your future in peace. A boundary is flexible, movable, and is based off **YOUR** discretion. Your heart space should be earned and not freely given. Therefore, if people have hurt you in your past relationships, what boundary will you hold with them? Somehow, our ego, our pride will have us to cut people off and not even tell them the reason why they are cut off from your life. Effective communication and boundary-setting skills are needed so the person can have self- awareness of how this experience affected you. If this individual keep doing things to disrespect or offend you after you have spoken your truth assertively. Then, you can kick them to the curve (in love). What happens when you been hurt so bad that your heart turns cold and you become emotionally numb? What happens if you want the wall to stay up?

That is a dangerous place to be. The reason why I say that is because when an individual loses feeling-- they lose compassion towards themselves and others. If you can imagine it is almost like a person walking around like the tin man on the Wizard of Oz. The Tin Man did not have a heart nor a brain. Are you a walking Tin Man?

Self- Reflective Questions

1. Are you operating from a wall or a boundary in your current relationships?
2. What stops you from being in the present moment with your emotions?
3. Do you have a hardened heart?

Journal Entry

Chapter 4

Unpacking the emotional baggage

"The time has come to let down your emotional baggage and walk towards freedom"

Emotional Baggage: can be described as insecurities that an individual carries over from previous experience.

Emotional Baggage is the epitome of broken relationships. Often in childhood, if we had a traumatic experience and it has not been processed, an individual will present themselves as an adult that has anger outburst "Temper tantrums." Ultimately, the individual is dealing with hurt little boy or girl within them. The emotional baggage can manifest in anxiety or fear of rejection. A relationship can be going perfectly well, and the individual will start an argument to cause a rift in the relationship to sabotage the relationship because their minds have conditioned them that the relationship was going to end anyway. Emotional Baggage also connects to the lack of self-awareness. How can you be married for five times and the individual never own up to the fact that you had a part to play in the relationship ending?

I love using metaphors in counseling and my personal life. The metaphor I often use for the situation is a baby having a soiled diaper and the mother takes the diaper off without wiping the baby down. This is how individuals are when they jump from relationship to relationship without processing the intense emotions from the previous life experience. I want to encourage you to self-reflect and heal so you can break generational curses of family members carrying emotional baggage in your bloodline.

Self-Reflective Questions

1. Do you have emotional baggage?

2. If so, how is it manifesting in your relationships?

3. Are you ready to release the emotional baggage?

Journal Entry

Chapter 5

Watch your words

"Be careful about what you say, once you release it sorry cannot take back the pain of what was said"

Effective Communication Skills: The skill set that shows the ability to engage properly in communication with others.

In the words of my loving adopted mother, Mrs. Denise Floyd, " I am a survivor, that's what I do, in some aspect of this life we need people, I rather just use words to build you up and uplift you versus tear them down that is my gift to humankind ". On the other hand, my adopted father, Dr. Russell Floyd, he is not so sweet with his words, for instance, "Damn it the hell". He will cruse at you and tell you the full unadulterated truth. Both aspects of communication I cherish because I receive feedback and insight into my life through both. Often, in our interaction with people, we negate to be in tune with how our words affect people. Our words can either tear down or build up the people that are connected to us. Unfortunately, if an individual is raised with a family of people being verbally abusive. What happens when this individual grows up to be an adult and he or she becomes verbally abusive to their spouse and children? Do hurt people continue to hurt people?

I want to encourage you to stay true to how you are. If you tell your truth without no sugar or chaser, or you put a lot of sugar and icing on your truth, I want you to practice something for me. Before you open your mouth, I want you to ask yourself this question? Will I offend myself with the truth I am about to release? Is this truth going to edify and grow this person or tear them down and hurt them? These are powerful self -reflective questions to ask ourselves to enhance our effective communication skills and strengthen our relationships.

Self- Reflective Questions

1. How do you communicate your truth?
2. Do you ever step back and process your truth before you say it?
3. Have you ever regretted saying something to someone and the consequence was that it ended the relationship?

Journal Entry

Chapter 6
Conclusion

In reading my first book, my earnest hope is that you gain some form of inspiration, wisdom, and enlightenment. The reason why I decided to write about this topic was because of my best friend, I was having this intense phone conversation about dating, marriage, and being frustrated with the African American brother. She was telling me her truth about her current relationship dynamics and conflict and she stated something that hit me like a ton of bricks. She stated that "Friend, I been hurt so bad by the men in my life to the point of where my walls I cannot break". I kept silent for a minute because at that moment, to be transparent with you, I understood her emotional pain. Immediately, I grabbed my journal and began to write. My truth is that I have been married and I was in love with the illusion of a man versus the reality of a man that he was, and I lost my father, who was the soul of what real man was. Fast forward, I had to allow myself the space to heal from these experiences. It has been an interesting journey, but I have learned the importance of building relationships with others and growing to love people unconditionally. I encourage each person reading this book to do your soul work by spiritual, mentally and physically getting in tune with yourself, and find a great mental health therapist and process your past and present traumatic experiences, so you can let go of the emotional baggage and

LIVE YOUR LIFE!

Wounded Healer

A piece of my heart left me on January 14, 2015, I found ways to survive and cope.

Yet underneath the mask, there lays tears of pain and hurt because my mind floods with memories of you. Through my grief work, I have learned to not focus on you not being here, but I will focus on how

I can continue your legacy to let you live forever. I have found the remedy, Dad. Every time I sit in front of someone, who has lost someone special to them, I have a place to minister from to acknowledge the pain they are experiencing, and I let them know that it will get better. As we take this journey from a different perspective, a different mindset. The wounded healer speaks..........

References

Duran, E. (2006). Healing the soul wound: counseling with American Indians and other native peoples. New York: Teachers College Press.

Sadeghi, H. (2019). Clarity Cleanse: 12 steps to finding renewed energy, spiritual fulfillment, and emotional... healing. S.l.: Grand Central Publishing

Definitions were derived from the Merriam-Webster Dictionary.

King James Version Bible

Who am I? Exercise

"I" Statements   Exercise

Current self-versus Ideal Self

Who am I?

Draw a circle in the middle of the page. Write positive characteristics of yourself inside the circle and negative characteristics outside the circle.

"I "statements

Reflective listening is an essential component of communication. Where you use an "I" statement it gives people self-awareness on how you feel. Think about a recent situation that made you angry. Write out I feel…… explain the reason you feel that way and why.

The current self-versus reality of self

Draw a vertical line in the middle of the page and one side. Describe where you are currently on one side of the line and on the other side describe where you want to be.

www.ingramcontent.com/pod-product-compliance
Lightning Source LLC
Chambersburg PA
CBHW022009100426
42736CB00041B/1431